THE MEDITERRANEAN DIET FOR TWO

Unlocking the Secrets of a Balanced Lifestyle.

Easy and Healthy Recipes That Everyone Can Enjoy

Reed Kellan

TABLE OF CONTENTS

INTRODUCTION

"Love yourself enough to live a healthy lifestyle."

Are you feeling overwhelmed by the idea of following a healthy lifestyle? You might think that it requires too much time, money, and sacrificing taste - but it doesn't have to be that way. The Mediterranean diet is one of the most popular diets around and it offers many benefits. Unlike other diets, it's not just about restricting calories or sacrificing good food. It's about making healthy lifestyle choices, including eating fresh seafood, vegetables, nuts, fruits and herbs. Plus, there are many exercises and spiritual awareness activities included as well.

Starting a diet can be difficult if you try to go at it alone; cravings can get the best of us when we don't have anyone else to keep us motivated. That's why sharing your dieting journey with someone else can help make things easier and more enjoyable. This Mediterranean Diet Cookbook for Two will give you delicious recipes to share with your significant other that won't take longer than 30 minutes to prepare - so no stale leftovers here! Enjoy fresh meals every day while working together towards a healthier lifestyle.`

CHAPTER 1 : BREAKFAST

MANGO SMOOTHIE BOWL

Total Time: 10 minutes

Servings: 2

Ingredients

- 1 cup mangoes, frozen
- ½ cup mangoes, fresh
- 2 tablespoons sliced walnuts
- 2 teaspoons chia seeds
- 1 ½ tablespoon protein powder, flavored
- 1 teaspoon maple syrup, unsweetened
- 2 tablespoons softened cashew butter, unsalted
- ¼ cup coconut granola
- ½ cup coconut milk, unsweetened
- 1 teaspoon ground nutmeg

How to Make:

1. Place the frozen mangoes, protein powder, cashew butter, maple syrup and coconut milk into a blender and blend until it is smooth.
2. Divide the mixture between two serving bowls.
3. Sprinkle over the walnuts, chia seeds, coconut granola and nutmeg before serving.

Nutritional Information Per Serving:

Cal; 370 Total Fats: 17 g; Saturated Fat: 2.5 g; Carbohydrate: 32 g; Sugar: 16 g; Fiber: 7 g; Protein: 25 g;

CARROT CAKE SMOOTHIE BOWL

Total Time: 10 minutes

Servings: 2

Ingredients

- 2 large carrots, sliced
- 1 frozen banana
- ¼ teaspoon ground cinnamon
- ¼ cup rolled oats, gluten-free
- ½ teaspoon baking powder, gluten-free
- 2 tablespoons almond butter, unsalted
- ½ cup almond milk, unsweetened

How to Make:

1. Place the carrots and banana into a blender and blend until it is a smooth consistency.
2. Add the oats, cinnamon, baking powder and almond butter to the blender and blend for another few seconds.
3. Slowly add in the almond milk until desired consistency is reached.
4. Divide the mixture between two serving bowls and enjoy!

Nutritional Information Per Serving:

Cal; 310 Total Fats: 15 g; Saturated Fat: 2 g; Carbohydrate: 42 g; Sugar: 16 g; Fiber: 7 g; Protein: 10 g;

#BLUEBERRY BANANA SMOOTHIE BOWL

Total Time: 7 minutes

Servings: 2

Ingredients

- 1 cup frozen blueberries
- 1 banana, peeled, frozen
- ¼ teaspoon ground cinnamon
- ¼ cup rolled oats, gluten-free
- ½ teaspoon baking powder, gluten free
- 2 tablespoons peanut butter, unsalted
- ½ cup almond milk, unsweetened

How to Make:

1. Place the blueberries and banana into a blender and blend until it is a smooth consistency.
2. Add the oats, cinnamon, baking powder and peanut butter to the blender and blend for another few seconds.
3. Slowly add in the almond milk until desired consistency is reached.
4. Divide the mixture between two serving bowls and enjoy!

Nutritional Information Per Serving:

Cal; 310 Total Fats: 15 g; Saturated Fat: 2 g; Carbohydrate: 42 g; Sugar: 16 g; Fiber: 7 g; Protein: 10 g;

CHERRY ALMOND SMOOTHIE BOWL

Total Time: 7 minutes

Servings: 2

Ingredients

- 1 cup frozen cherries
- 1 banana, peeled, frozen
- ¼ teaspoon almond extract
- ¼ cup rolled oats, gluten-free
- ½ teaspoon baking powder, gluten free
- 2 tablespoons almond butter, unsalted
- ½ cup coconut milk, unsweetened

How to Make:

1. Place the cherries and banana into a blender and blend until it is a smooth consistency.
2. Add the oats, almond extract, baking powder and almond butter to the blender and blend for another few seconds.
3. Slowly add in the coconut milk until desired consistency is reached.
4. Divide the mixture between two serving bowls and enjoy!

Nutritional Information Per Serving:

Cal; 315 Total Fats: 15 g; Saturated Fat: 5 g; Carbohydrate: 43 g; Sugar: 19 g; Fiber: 6 g; Protein: 8 g;

MORNING JUICE BOWL

Total Time: 5 minutes

Servings: 2

Ingredients

- 1 banana, peeled, frozen
- ¼ cup wheatgrass powder
- ½ cup fresh orange juice
- ¼ teaspoon turmeric powder
- ½ teaspoon ground ginger

How to Make:

1. Place the banana into a blender and blend until creamy.
2. Add in the wheatgrass powder, orange juice, turmeric powder and ground ginger and blend for another few seconds.
3. Divide the mixture between two serving bowls and enjoy!

Nutritional Information Per Serving:

Cal; 103 Total Fats: 0 g; Saturated Fat: 0 g; Carbohydrate: 26 g; Sugar: 13 g; Fiber: 3 g; Protein: 3g

CHAI SPICE SMOOTHIE

Total Time: 5 minutes

Servings: 2

Ingredients

- 1 banana, peeled, frozen
- ½ cup chai spice tea, brewed and cooled
- 1 cup almond milk, unsweetened
- ⅓ cup oats

How to Make:

1. Place the banana, chai spice tea, almond milk and oats into a blender and blend until creamy.
2. Divide the mixture between two serving glasses and enjoy!

Nutritional Information Per Serving:

Cal; 230 Total Fats: 4.5 g; Saturated Fat: 0.7 g; Carbohydrate: 39 g; Sugar: 12 g; Fiber: 6g; Protein: 8g

AVOCADO TOAST

Total Time: 15 minutes

Servings: 2

Ingredients –

- 2 medium tomatoes, sliced
- ½ cup basil, fresh
- 1 medium avocado, peeled, pitted, sliced
- ½ medium green sweet pepper, sliced
- ½ teaspoon ground black pepper, divided
- 4 olives, pitted and sliced
- ½ cup arugula, fresh
- 2 teaspoons minced garlic
- 2 large slices of bread, whole wheat
- ¼ teaspoon salt
- 2 eggs at room temperature

How to Make:

1. Take a medium non-stick frying pan and place over medium heat. When hot, place the bread slices in the pan and toast on both sides until golden in color. Transfer the toasted bread slices onto a cutting board and cool at room temperature.

2. In a medium bowl add the eggs and salt and whisk until well mixed. Pour the mixture into the frying pan and stir until scrambled and cooked. Set aside in a small bowl when done.

3. Place avocado slices evenly on top of the toasted bread slices and then add garlic on top; mash with a fork to spread across toast. Then place tomato slices, sweet pepper slices, arugula leaves, basil leaves, olives and prepared scrambled eggs evenly on top of each slice of toast; sprinkle black pepper on top to finish off. Place prepared avocado toast onto serving plate and serve!

Nutritional Information Per Serving:

Cal; 618 Total Fats: 25 g; Saturated Fat: 5 g; Carbohydrate: 87 g; Sugar: 29 g; Fiber: 24 g; Protein: 27 g;

TACO SALAD

Total Time: 15 minutes

Servings: 2

Ingredients :

- 1 cup cooked linguine, divided
- ½ medium red onion, chopped -
- 1 large tomato, diced
- 2 tablespoons olive oil
- ¼ teaspoon ground black pepper
- ½ teaspoon garlic powder
- 1 tablespoon lime juice
- ¾ teaspoons chili powder
- 4 medium lettuce leaves, torn into pieces
- 2 tablespoons salsa
- ½ cup canned black beans, rinsed and drained

How to Make:

1. Take a medium pot and place over high heat. When hot, add the linguine and cook according to package instructions. When done, remove from heat and drain well. Divide the cooked linguine into two equal portions and set aside.
2. In a medium bowl combine the red onion, tomato, olive oil, black pepper, garlic powder and lime juice; mix together until blended; set aside. Place a medium nonstick frying pan over medium heat.
3. When hot pour in the prepared onion mixture; cook for 3 minutes or until vegetables are tender stirring occasionally.
4. Add chili powder to finish off; transfer onto a plate when done. Place lettuce leaves on top of one of the reserved cooked linguine portions; add bean salsa followed by fried onion mixture evenly on top of lettuce leaves; finally place remaining half portion of cooked linguine on top to form tacos shells layers. Top taco shell with salsa and serve!

Nutritional Information Per Serving:

Cal; 336 Total Fats: 18 g; Saturated Fat: 2 g; Carbohydrate: 38 g Fiber: 10 g ; Protein 7g

EGGPLANT & CHEESE PIZZA

Total Time: 25 minutes

Servings: 2

Ingredients

- ½ cup canned tomato sauce, divided
- 1 large eggplant, thinly sliced into rounds
- ½ teaspoon salt
- ½ cup shredded mozzarella cheese
- 2 tablespoons olive oil
- ¼ teaspoon red pepper flakes

How to Cook:

1. Preheat oven to 400ºF. Take a medium baking sheet and line with parchment paper; spread one tablespoon of tomato sauce over the baking sheet.
2. Arrange the sliced eggplant on top of the tomato sauce and brush each round with olive oil on both sides; sprinkle salt generously over them as well.
3. Transfer into preheated oven and bake for 15 minutes or until golden brown in color.
4. Remove from oven and set aside. Place a small frying pan over medium heat; pour remaining tomato sauce into the pan and cook for 3 minutes stirring occasionally; add red pepper flakes during last minute of cooking time before turning off stovetop burner.
5. To assemble pizza; top cooked eggplant rounds with mozzarella cheese & prepared homemade pizza sauce then transfer back onto preheated oven & bake at 375ºF for 5 minutes or until cheese is melted & bubbly!

Nutritional Information Per Serving:

Cal; 341 Total Fats: 18 g ; Saturated Fat: 5 g Carbohydrate: 22 g ; Sugar: 9 g Fiber 4 g Protein 13g

SPINACH & FETA SCRAMBLED EGGS

Total Time: 10 minutes

Servings: 2

Ingredients -

- 1 tablespoon olive oil
- 1 cup baby spinach
- ¼ teaspoon ground black pepper
- ½ cup diced tomatoes
- ¼ teaspoon salt
- 4 large eggs, at room temperature

How to Cook:

1. Heat a large nonstick pan over medium heat and add the oil. When hot, add spinach and diced tomatoes and sauté for 1 minute. 2. Crack the eggs into the pan and stir constantly for 30 seconds or until scrambled then add feta cheese, pepper and salt; cook until all ingredients are blended together evenly & eggs have set. 3. Spoon prepared scramble onto two plates & serve with sourdough toast! Enjoy!

Nutritional Information Per Serving:

Cal; 199 Total Fats: 16 g ; Saturated Fat: 5 g Carbohydrate: 2.4 g ; Sugar: 1.4 g Fiber 4 g Protein 11.5g

CHEESY POTATO SCRAMBLE

Total Time: 20 minutes

Servings: 4

Ingredients

- 2 tablespoons olive oil
- 1 diced onion
- 4 cups diced Yukon gold potatoes
- ¼ teaspoon ground black pepper
- 1 cup shredded cheddar cheese
- ½ teaspoon garlic powder
- 4 large eggs, whisked, at room temperature

How to Cook:

1. Heat a large nonstick skillet over medium heat and add the oil. When hot, add the diced onion and sauté for 5 minutes or until softened.
2. Add potatoes to the pan; season with pepper then cover & cook for 10 minutes or until softened stirring occasionally.
3. Pour in whisked eggs; sprinkle garlic powder over then scramble until cooked through before folding in shredded cheese & reducing heat to low.
4. Cover & cook an additional 3 minutes or until cheese has melted & eggs have set before serving warm! Enjoy!

Nutritional Information Per Serving:

Cal; 219 Total Fats: 14 g ; Saturated Fat: 6 g Carbohydrate; 13 g ; Sugar: 1 g Fiber 1 g Protein 12g

ZESTY POTATO FRITTERS

Total Time: 20 minutes

Servings: 4

Ingredients

- 2 tablespoons olive oil
- 1 diced onion
- 4 cups diced Yukon gold potatoes
- ¼ teaspoon ground black pepper
- 1 cup shredded cheddar cheese
- ½ teaspoon garlic powder
- 4 large eggs, whisked, at room temperature

How to Cook:

1. Heat a large nonstick skillet over medium heat and add the oil. When hot, add the diced onion and sauté for 5 minutes or until softened.
2. 2. Add potatoes to the pan; season with pepper then stir until coated in oil & cook for 10 minutes or until softened stirring occasionally.
3. 3. In a medium bowl whisk together eggs & garlic powder before pouring into the potato mixture; continue to stir & scramble until cooked through before folding in shredded cheese & reducing heat to low.
4. 4. Cover & cook an additional 3 minutes or until cheese has melted before serving warm! Enjoy!

Nutritional Information Per Serving:

Cal; 219 Total Fats: 14 g ; Saturated Fat: 6 g Carbohydrate; 13 g ; Sugar: 1 g Fiber 1 g Protein 12g

TASTY POTATO TACOS

Total Time: 20 minutes

Servings: 2

Ingredients

- 2 tablespoons olive oil
- 1 diced onion
- 4 cups diced Yukon gold potatoes
- -¼ teaspoon ground black pepper
- 1 cup shredded Monterey Jack cheese
- ½ teaspoon garlic powder
- 4 soft taco shells

How to Cook:

1. In a large nonstick skillet, heat the oil over medium heat. Add the onion and sauté for 5 minutes or until softened.
2. 2. Add potatoes to the pan and season with pepper then stir until coated in oil & cook for 10 minutes or until softened stirring occasionally.
3. 3. Reduce heat to low and fold in shredded cheese before covering & cooking an additional 3 minutes or until melted.
4. 4. Serve the potato mixture in warm taco shells & enjoy!

Nutritional Information Per Serving:

Cal; 412 Total Fats: 16 g ; Saturated Fat: 7 g Carbohydrate; 34 g ; Sugar: 1 g Fiber 4 g Protein 24g

CREAMY POTATO FRITTERS

Total Time: 15 minutes

Servings: 2

Ingredients

- 2 tablespoons olive oil
- 1 diced onion
- 4 cups diced Yukon gold potatoes
- ¼ teaspoon ground black pepper
- 1 cup shredded Monterey Jack cheese
- ½ cup Parmesan cheese, grated

How to Cook:

1. In a large nonstick skillet, heat the oil over medium heat. Add the onion and sauté for 5 minutes or until softened. 2. Add potatoes to the pan and season with pepper then stir until coated in oil & cook for 10 minutes or until softened stirring occasionally. 3. Transfer potato mixture to a bowl & fold in both cheeses before forming golf ball size patties with your hands. 4. Heat an additional tablespoon of oil in skillet before adding potato patties, cooking around 3 minutes per side or until golden brown & crispy! Serve warm!

Nutritional Information Per Serving:

Cal; 413 Total Fats: 20 g ; Saturated Fat: 9 g Carbohydrate; 26 g ; Sugar; 1 g Fiber 4 g Protein 25g

EGG AND CHEDDAR SCRAMBLE

Total Time: 10 minutes

Servings: 2

Ingredients

- 1 tablespoon olive oil
- 2 cups diced Yukon gold potatoes
- ¼ teaspoon ground black pepper
- 1 cup shredded Cheddar cheese
- 2 large eggs, beaten

How to Cook:

1. In a nonstick skillet, heat the oil over medium. Add the potatoes and season with pepper then cook for 8 minutes or until softened stirring occasionally.
2. Push aside the potatoes and pour in the eggs before stirring until just set, about 1 minute.
3. Gently fold in the shredded Cheddar cheese before dividing onto two plates & serve!

Nutritional Information Per Serving:

Cal; 444 Total Fats; 20 g Saturated Fat; 9 g Carbohydrate; 27 g Sugar; 1 Fiber 4 g Protein 25g

CHAPTER 2 :
LUNCH

CHICKPEA AND OLIVE SALAD

Total Time: 15 minutes

Servings: 2

Ingredients

- ½ cup diced cucumbers
- ⅛ teaspoon garlic powder
- ½ cup quartered cherry tomatoes
- ⅛ teaspoon ground black pepper
- ¼ cup chopped parsley, fresh
- 3 tablespoons chopped onion
- ⅛ teaspoon salt
- 3 tablespoons halved kalamata olives
- 7 ounces chickpeas, canned, rinsed
- 1 tablespoon olive oil
- 3 tablespoons crumbled feta cheese
- 2 tablespoons red wine vinegar

How to Cook:

1. Whisk together the vinegar, olive oil, garlic powder, black pepper and salt in a large bowl.
2. Add the tomatoes, cucumbers, onions, olives, parsley and feta to the mixture before tossing everything together until evenly coated.
3. Divide onto two plates & serve.

Nutritional Information Per Serving:

Cal; 256 Total Fats; 14 g Saturated Fat; 3 g Carbohydrate 24 g Sugar 3 g Fiber 5 g Protein 9g

AVOCADO AND CORN SALAD

Total Time: 15 minutes

Servings: 2

Ingredients

- 5 ounces canned corn
- 1 tablespoon olive oil
- 1 cup baby spinach
- ½ medium purple cabbage, torn
- 2 tablespoons chopped onion
- ½ cup halved cherry tomatoes
- 2 tablespoons sunflower seeds
- ½ cup chopped avocado
- 3 tablespoons honey mustard dressing

How to Cook:

1. Take a large bowl and add the corn, tomatoes, onion, and avocado. Stir until everything is well-combined.
2. Add in the spinach, cabbage and sunflower seeds before stirring all ingredients together until everything is evenly mixed.
3. Drizzle in the olive oil and honey mustard dressing over the mixture before stirring once more to ensure everything is evenly coated.
4. Pour the salad into a serving bowl and enjoy!

Nutritional Information Per Serving:

Calories; 432 Total Fats; 32 g Saturated Fat; 5 g Carbohydrate 17 g Sugar 8 g Fiber 7 g Protein 20g

DELICIOUS QUINOA SALAD

Satisfy your cravings with a quick and easy quinoa salad that's packed with flavour. All it takes is 20 minutes for two servings. Here's what you'll need:

Ingredients

- 1 ½ cup baby spinach
- 7 ounces canned chickpeas, rinsed
- 1 cup sliced cucumber
- ¾ teaspoon dijon mustard
- ⅓ cup sliced onion
- ½ cup halved cherry tomatoes
- 3 teaspoons chopped fresh oregano
- ¼ cup halved kalamata olives
- ¾ teaspoon honey sweetener
- 1 ½ cups cooked quinoa, cooled
- ⅛ teaspoon crushed red pepper
- ¼ cup olive oil
- ½ cup crumbled feta cheese, divided
- 3 tablespoons red wine vinegar

How to Cook:

1. In a large bowl, combine the vinegar, honey, oregano, mustard, red pepper and oil and whisk until smooth.
2. Mix in the quiona, chickpeas, spinach, cucumber, onion and tomatoes until everything is evenly coated with dressing. Cover the bowl and refrigerate for 30 minutes.
3. Add in the olives and ¼ of the feta cheese before spooning into individual serving bowls. Top each off with remaining feta cheese for extra flavour! Nutritional Information

Per Serving: Calories;

472 Total Fats; 30 g Saturated Fat; 7 g Carbohydrate 39 g Sugar 7.4 g Fiber 6.9 g Protein 12 g

TUNA AND WHITE BEAN SALAD

This light, summery salad can be thrown together in no time. Perfect for a lunch or quick snack on the go! Here's what you'll need:

Ingredients

- 2 cans of tuna in water, drained
- 1 can of white beans, rinsed
- ¼ cup diced red onion
- ¼ cup diced celery
- ¾ cup Greek yogurt
- ½ teaspoon dried dill weed
- Freshly cracked black pepper to taste

How to Make:

1. In a large bowl, combine the tuna, white beans, onion, celery and yogurt until everything is evenly mixed.
2. Add the dill weed and pepper to taste before stirring again.
3. Serve chilled or at room temperature. Enjoy!

Nutritional Information Per Serving:

Calories; 183 Total Fats; 5 g Saturated Fat; 0 g Carbohydrate 16 g Sugar 7 g Fiber 6 g Protein 22 g

AVOCADO EGG SALAD SANDWICH

This easy-to-assemble sandwich is both delicious and packed with protein. Plus, it takes only minutes to put together! Here's what you need:

Ingredients

- 2 large eggs
- 1 ripe avocado, peeled, pitted, mashed
- 4 whole wheat bread slices
- ½ teaspoon garlic powder
- ¼ cup diced red onion
- Salt and freshly cracked black pepper to taste

How to Make:

1. Boil the eggs for 8 minutes until hard boiled then leave aside to cool. When cooled, peel and mash.
2. In a separate bowl combine the mashed egg with avocado and mix until everything is evenly combined. Add in garlic powder and diced onion before seasoning with salt and pepper.
3. Spread the egg salad across two bread slices before topping each with another slice of bread. Serve chilled or at room temperature without delay!

Nutritional Information Per Serving:

Calories; 286 Total Fats; 14 g Saturated Fat; 3 g Carbohydrate 29 g Sugar 2 g Fiber 5 g Protein 12 g

GRILLED CHICKEN AND AVOCADO SALAD

This easy-to-assemble salad is both tasty and packed with essential nutrients. Plus, it takes only minutes to make! Here's what you need:

Ingredients

- 2 boneless, skinless chicken breasts
- 1 ripe avocado, peeled, pitted, diced
- 4 cups romaine lettuce
- ½ teaspoon garlic powder
- ¼ cup diced red onion
- Salt and freshly cracked black pepper to taste

How to Make:

1. Preheat the grill or stovetop grill pan over a high heat for about five minutes until hot. Rub the chicken breasts with garlic powder before adding salt and pepper to taste. Place onto the heated grilling surface and cook for 4 minutes per side or until cooked through.
2. In a separate bowl combine the diced avocado and romaine lettuce before mixing in garlic powder, diced onion and add salt and pepper to taste.
3. Cut each chicken breast into strips before adding them into the prepared salad. Serve immediately without delay!

Nutritional Information Per Serving:

Calories; 230 Total Fats; 9 g Saturated Fat; 1 g Carbohydrate 17 g Sugar 2 g Fiber 7g Protein 24 g

CHICKEN AND SWEET POTATO SALAD

This delicious dish is packed with heart-healthy ingredients and is sure to leave you feeling satisfied. Plus, it takes just minutes to make! Here's what you need:

Ingredients

- 2 boneless, skinless chicken breasts
- 6 cups shredded sweet potato
- ½ teaspoon garlic powder
- ¼ cup diced red onion
- 1 tablespoon olive oil
- Salt and freshly cracked black pepper to taste

How to Make:

1. Preheat the oven or stovetop grill pan over a high heat for about five minutes until hot. Rub the chicken breasts with garlic powder before adding salt and pepper to taste. Place onto the heated grilling surface and cook for 4 minutes per side or until cooked through.
2. Toss together the shredded sweet potatoes, red onion, olive oil, and season the mix with salt and pepper to taste. Spread evenly in an oven-safe baking dish and bake in preheated oven for about 25 minutes or until golden brown.
3. Cut each chicken breast into strips before adding them into the prepared salad. Serve immediately without delay!

Nutritional Information Per Serving: Calories

340 Total Fats; 9 g Saturated Fat; 1 g Carbohydrate 48 g Sugar 8 g Fiber 6g Protein 23 g

SPICY SHRIMP AND AVOCADO RICE BOWL

This tasty combination of flavors is sure to tantalize your taste buds. Plus, it takes minimal effort to make! Here's what you need:

Ingredients

- 1 lb shrimp, peeled and deveined
- 2 tablespoons olive oil
- Salt and freshly cracked black pepper to taste
- 2 cloves garlic, minced
- 1 teaspoon ground cumin
- 2 teaspoons chili powder
- 2 cups cooked white or brown rice
- ½ cup frozen corn kernels, thawed
- 2 avocados, diced
- 1 tablespoon fresh lime juice

How to Make:

1. Preheat the stovetop grill pan over a medium heat for about five minutes until hot. Rub the shrimp with salt and pepper before adding them onto the heated grilling surface. Grill for 2 minutes per side or until the flesh is pink and slightly charred.
2. Heat a large skillet over medium heat and add olive oil. Add the garlic, cumin, chili powder and cook for about 30 seconds stirring constantly until fragrant. Add in cooked rice followed by corn kernels and stir fry for about 5 minutes until everything is evenly incorporated together.
3. To serve – scoop out portions of the spicy shrimp grilled rice mix into appropriate serving bowls before topping with cubed avocado pieces in each bowl before adding a squeeze of fresh lime juice on top!

Nutritional Information Per Serving:

Calories; 400 Total Fats; 18 g Saturated Fat; 3 g Carbohydrate 41 g Sugar 4 g Fiber 8g Protein 22 g

CARAMELIZED ONION, PEACH AND AVOCADO SALAD

This flavorful salad is great for a light lunch or dinner. It's refreshing, healthy and takes only minutes to whip up! Here's what you need:

Ingredients

- 1 tablespoon olive oil
- 1 small white onion, peeled and thinly sliced
- 2 ripe peaches, pitted and sliced
- 2 avocados, diced
- Salt and freshly cracked black pepper to taste

How to Make:

1. Heat the olive oil in a large skillet over medium heat. Add in the sliced onion before cooking them down until they become caramelized - this should take roughly 7 minutes.
2. Place the cooked onions onto a plate before adding in the diced avocado pieces then topping with peach slices on top of it all. Season with salt and freshly cracked black pepper if desired before serving.

Nutritional Information Per Serving:

Calories; 222 Total Fats; 14 g Saturated Fat; 2 g Carbohydrate 21 g Sugar 10 g Fiber 8g Protein 4 g

GREEN BEAN, COCONUT AND TURMERIC SALAD

This flavorful salad is packed full of healthy ingredients and will be sure to satisfy even the pickiest of eaters. Plus, it takes only minutes to make! Here's what you need:

Ingredients

- 2 cups cooked green beans, cut into bite-sized pieces
- 1 cup coconut flakes
- 1 teaspoon ground turmeric
- Salt and freshly cracked black pepper to taste

How to Make:

1. Place the cooked green beans into a bowl before sprinkling with the coconut flakes and ground turmeric. Toss everything together until evenly mixed. Season with salt and freshly cracked pepper if desired before serving.
2. Serve this vibrant salad as a side dish, or in a wrap for a delicious and healthy lunch/dinner!

Nutritional Information Per Serving:

Calories; 208 Total Fats; 17 g Saturated Fat; 16 g Carbohydrate 5 g Sugar 4 g Fiber 7g Protein 5 g

GARLIC HERB ROASTED POTATOES

This easy recipe is a delicious and healthy way to satisfy your potato cravings. The roasted potatoes are full of flavor thanks to herbs and garlic, making them a perfect side dish for any meal! Here's what you need:

Ingredients

- 2 large potatoes (sliced into bite-sized pieces)
- 4 cloves of garlic (minced)
- 3 tablespoons olive oil
- 2 teaspoons dried basil
- 1 teaspoon dried oregano
- ½ teaspoon salt

How to Make:

1. Preheat the oven to 400 degrees Fahrenheit and line a baking sheet with parchment paper. Place the sliced potatoes onto the prepared baking sheet before drizzling with olive oil, minced garlic, basil, oregano and salt. Mix everything together evenly until the potatoes are completely coated in herbs and spices.
2. Bake in preheated oven for 30 minutes, flipping halfway through cooking time so that both sides get golden brown in color. Serve warm and enjoy!

Nutritional Information Per Serving:

Calories; 105 Total Fats; 7 g Saturated Fat; 1 g Carbohydrate 10 g Sugar 1g Fiber 2g Protein 2g

ZUCCHINI RICOTTA STUFFED SHELLS

This easy-to-make and delicious stuffed shells recipe has become a family favorite in no time! Filled with ricotta, zucchini and herbs, this dish is packed with flavor and sure to impress everyone at the dinner table. Here's what you need:

Ingredients

- 12 jumbo pasta shells (cooked and cooled)
- 1 cup ricotta cheese
- ½ cup grated Parmesan cheese
- 2 cloves garlic (minced)
- ½ teaspoon salt
- ½ teaspoon dried oregano
- ¼ teaspoon freshly ground black pepper
- 2 cups zucchini, grated

How to Make:

1. Preheat the oven to 350 degrees Fahrenheit before combining the ricotta cheese, Parmesan cheese, garlic, salt, oregano and pepper in a bowl. Mix together until everything is evenly combined before stirring in cilantro and zucchini.

2. Place six cooked pasta shells on the bottom of an oven safe baking dish. Spoon some of the ricotta mixture into each shell before topping each with remaining shells. Sprinkle the top layer of shells with Parmesan cheese before baking for about 30 minutes or until lightly golden brown in color. Serve warm and enjoy!

Nutritional Information Per Serving:

Calories; 150 Total Fats; 7 g Saturated Fat; 3 g Carbohydrate 15 g Sugar 1g Fiber 2g Protein 10g

TURKEY STUFFED PEPPERS

These tasty and nutritious Turkey Stuffed Peppers are perfect for a quick and healthy weeknight dinner. Packed with lean ground turkey, vegetables, quinoa, and herbs, these peppers are sure to be a hit with the whole family. Here's what you need:

Ingredients

- 2 bell peppers (halved lengthwise and seeded)
- 1 teaspoon olive oil
- ½ onion (diced)
- ½ cup celery (diced)
- 1 garlic clove (minced)
- 2 cups cooked quinoa
- 1 lb lean ground turkey
- ½ cup green peas
- ¼ teaspoon dried oregano

How to Make:

1. Preheat the oven to 350 degrees Fahrenheit before adding olive oil to a large skillet over medium heat. Add the onions, celery and garlic then sauté until everything is softened. Stir in the cooked quinoa, ground turkey, peas and oregano then cook until the meat is no longer pink.
2. Place pepper halves in an oven safe baking dish before stuffing them with the mixture from Step 1. Bake in preheated oven for 20 minutes or until lightly golden brown in color on top. Serve warm and enjoy!

Nutritional Information Per Serving:

Calories; 264 Total Fats; 8 g Saturated Fat; 3 g Carbohydrate 16g Sugar 4g Fiber 6g Protein 24g

TASTE OF THE MEDITERRANEAN

This Taste of the Mediterranean dish is sure to pack a flavorful punch! With savory olives, onions, and feta cheese, plus healthy tomatoes and spinach for extra nutrition, you get it all with one delicious meal. Here's what you need:

Ingredients:

- 1 tablespoon olive oil
- 1 onion (diced)
- 2 cloves garlic (minced)
- 2 cups diced tomatoes
- ¼ cup pitted kalamata olives (chopped)
- ½ teaspoon oregano
- 3 cups baby spinach leaves
- ½ cup feta cheese (crumbled)

How to Make:

1. Begin by adding the olive oil to a large skillet over medium heat. Add the diced onion and minced garlic and sauté until softened. Add the diced tomatoes, kalamata olives and oregano before stirring in the spinach leaves. Cook until everything is heated through then stir in the crumbled feta cheese and serve warm. Enjoy! Nutritional Information

Per Serving:

Calories; 150 Total Fats; 8 g Saturated Fat; 3 g Carbohydrate 11g Sugar 5g Fiber 4g Protein 9g

MEDITERRANEAN FETA SALAD

This Mediterranean Feta Salad is the perfect refreshing summer side dish! With savory feta cheese, juicy tomatoes, crunchy cucumbers and fresh oregano, it's a flavor-packed dish that will have you coming back for more. Here's what you need:

Ingredients:

- 2 tablespoons olive oil
- 1 tablespoon lemon juice
- 1 clove garlic (minced)
- 1 teaspoon dried oregano leaves
- ¼ teaspoon salt
- ¼ teaspoon pepper
- 2 large tomatoes (diced)
- ½ cucumber (diced)
- ½ cup crumbled feta cheese

How to Make:

1. Combine the olive oil and lemon juice in a small bowl before whisking together along with the minced garlic, oregano leaves, salt and pepper.
2. In a separate bowl, gently toss together diced tomatoes, cucumbers and crumbled feta cheese. Drizzle the dressing over the tomato mixture before gently stirring until everything is evenly coated.
3. Serve chilled or at room temperature. Enjoy!

Nutritional Information Per Serving:

Calories; 110 Total Fats; 8 g Saturated Fat; 3 g Carbohydrate 4g Sugar 3g Fiber 1g Protein 5g

CHAPTER 3 : SNACK AND APPETIZER

CILANTRO LIME QUINOA

This Cilantro Lime Quinoa is a great way to add flavor and nutrition to your dinner plate. Full of fresh herbs and a zesty lime dressing, this hearty side dish is sure to be everyone's favorite! Here's what you need:

Ingredients:
- 1 cup uncooked quinoa
- 2 cups low-sodium vegetable broth
- 2 tablespoons extra virgin olive oil
- 2 teaspoon fresh lime juice
- 2 cloves garlic (minced)
- 1 tablespoon fresh cilantro (chopped)
- ½ teaspoon salt

How to Make:
1. Bring the vegetable broth and quinoa together in a medium saucepan before bringing it to a boil. Reduce the heat to low, cover the pan and simmer for 15 minutes or until the liquid is absorbed. Fluff with a fork before transferring into a large bowl.
2. In a small bowl whisk together the olive oil, lime juice, minced garlic, chopped cilantro, and salt until combined before pouring over the warm quinoa. Toss gently to combine before serving. Enjoy!

Nutritional Information Per Serving:
Calories; 215 Total Fats; 8 g Saturated Fat; 1g Carbohydrate 24 g Sugar 0 g Fiber 4 g Protein 7 g

GARLIC PARMESAN ROASTED BROCCOLI

This Garlic Parmesan Roasted Broccoli is an easy, healthy side dish that's full of flavor! The garlic and parmesan give it a delicious twist, making it perfect for any meal. Here's what you need:

Ingredients:

- 1 large head of broccoli (chopped into florets)
- 4 cloves garlic (minced)
- 2 tablespoons olive oil
- ¼ teaspoon salt
- ¼ cup shredded parmesan cheese

How to Make:

1. Preheat the oven to 400 degrees F (205 degrees C). Line a baking sheet with parchment paper and set aside. In a medium bowl combine the broccoli florets with minced garlic, olive oil, and salt before mixing until everything is evenly coated.
2. Transfer the seasoned broccoli onto the prepared baking sheet in a single layer then sprinkle with parmesan cheese before placing in preheated oven. Bake for 15 minutes or until golden brown, stirring occasionally so they cook evenly. Serve warm and enjoy!

Nutritional Information Per Serving:

Calories; 146 Total Fats; 10 g Saturated Fat; 3g Carbohydrate 7 g Sugar 0 g Fiber 3 g Protein 8 g

CURRY BUTTERNUT SQUASH SOUP

This Curry Butternut Squash Soup is a creamy and delicious soup perfect for cold nights! It's full of flavor from the curry powder, ginger and coconut milk, making it a comforting and healthy meal. Here's what you need:

Ingredients:

- 1 tablespoon olive oil
- 1 large onion (diced)
- 4 cloves garlic (minced)
- 2 teaspoons freshly grated ginger
- 1 teaspoon ground turmeric
- 3 teaspoons curry powder
- 6 cups chicken or vegetable broth
- 1 butternut squash (peeled & cubed)
- ½ can coconut milk

How to Make:

1. Heat the olive oil in a large pot over medium heat before adding the onion and garlic. Cook until softened and fragrant, stirring occasionally. Add the ginger, turmeric, curry powder, and broth then bring to boil. Once boiling reduce heat and add butternut squash. Simmer until squash is tender, about 10 minutes.
2. Remove from heat then use an immersion blender to puree the soup until smooth or transfer in batches to blender/food processor if desired. Add the coconut milk then season with salt & pepper to taste before serving hot!

Nutritional Information Per Serving:

Calories; 200 Total Fats; 13 g Saturated Fat; 10g Carbohydrate 15 g Sugar 5 g Fiber 3 g Protein 2 g

GLUTEN FREE CHOCOLATE CHIP COOKIES

These Gluten Free Chocolate Chip Cookies are a delicious and healthy treat! They're made without any wheat flour, but they still have the same chewy texture and chocolaty flavor that everyone loves. Here's what you need:

Ingredients:

- 2 cups almond flour
- 1 teaspoon baking soda
- ½ teaspoon salt
- ½ cup coconut oil, melted & cooled
- ½ cup honey
- 2 tablespoons flaxseed meal
- 1 teaspoon vanilla extract
- ½ cup dark chocolate chips

How to Make:

1. Preheat oven to 350F then line two baking sheets with parchment paper. In a medium mixing bowl, whisk together almond flour, baking soda and salt.
2. In a separate large mixing bowl, whisk together coconut oil, honey, flaxseed meal and vanilla until smooth. Add dry ingredients to wet ingredients in thirds until just combined then stir in chocolate chips.
3. Scoop cookie dough in tablespoon sized portions onto the prepared baking sheets then press down slightly before baking for 8 minutes or until golden brown on edges. Let cool before enjoying!

Nutritional Information Per Serving (1 cookie):

Calories; 121 Total Fats; 9 g Saturated Fat; 4g Carbohydrate 6 g Sugar 5 g Fiber 2 g Protein 2 g

COCONUT ALMOND OVERNIGHT OATS

These Coconut Almond Overnight Oats are a delicious and healthy breakfast that can be prepared in just minutes! They're full of creamy coconut, crunchy almonds and comforting oats for the perfect combination of flavors. Here's what you need:

Ingredients:

- 1 cup rolled oats
- 2 tablespoons chia seeds
- 1 cup unsweetened coconut milk
- 2 tablespoons honey
- ½ teaspoon ground cinnamon
- ¼ teaspoon almond extract
- ¼ cup almonds, chopped

How to Make:

1. In a jar or bowl, mix together oats, chia seeds, coconut milk, honey, cinnamon and almond extract until incorporated. Cover with a lid or plastic wrap then store in the refrigerator overnight.
2. When ready to eat in the morning, top oats with chopped almonds right before serving. Serve chilled or warmed up in microwave according to preference and enjoy!

Nutritional Information Per Serving (1 jar):

Calories; 321 Total Fats; 14 g Saturated Fat; 7g Carbohydrate 36 g Sugar 18 g Fiber 6 g Protein 8 g

CHAPTER 4 : DINNER

TACO BOWLS

These Taco Bowls are an easy and delicious dinner that everyone will love! Packed with delicious ingredients like quinoa, black beans, tomatoes and guacamole, they're sure to be a favorite in no time. Here's what you need:

Ingredients:

- 1 cup cooked quinoa
- ½ cup cooked black beans
- ½ cup diced tomatoes
- ½ cup fresh or frozen corn
- 1 avocado, mashed into guacamole
- 2 tablespoons olive oil
- Juice of 1 lemon
- ¼ teaspoon cumin
- Salt and pepper to taste

How to Make:

1. In a large bowl, mix together quinoa, black beans, tomatoes, and corn until incorporated.
2. In a separate small bowl, combine the guacamole ingredients by mashing the avocado with the olive oil, lemon juice, cumin, salt and pepper until creamy.
3. Divide quinoa mixture amongst two bowls and top each with half of the guacamole mixture. Serve immediately and enjoy!

Nutritional Information Per Serving (1 bowl):

Calories; 426 Total Fats; 28 g Saturated Fat; 4g Carbohydrate 44 g Sugar 8 g Fiber 11 g Protein 9 g

ONE POT CHILI MAC

This One Pot Chili Mac is a tasty and comforting dish that's sure to please the whole family. It's a great use of pantry staples, easy to make and ready in less than 30 minutes! Here's what you need:

Ingredients:

- 2 tablespoons olive oil
- 1 ¼ pounds ground beef
- ½ teaspoon onion powder
- 1 teaspoon garlic powder
- 1 teaspoon smoked paprika
- 1 teaspoon chili powder
- 1 teaspoon cumin
- ¼ cup tomato paste
- 2 cups chicken broth or vegetable broth for vegan option
- 8 ounces macaroni pasta shells or other small pasta shapes (uncooked)

How to Make:

1. Heat the olive oil in a large deep skillet over medium heat. Add the ground beef and cook, stirring occasionally, until cooked through.
2. Reduce heat to low then add the spices (onion powder, garlic powder, smoked paprika, chili powder, cumin) and stir for about 30 seconds until fragrant. Stir in tomato paste then add the broth and uncooked macaroni shells.
3. Bring to a simmer then reduce heat to low again and let simmer uncovered for 15 – 18 minutes or until most of the liquid has been absorbed by the pasta and its cooked al dente (firm but not overly so). Stir occasionally while it cooks if needed. Serve immediately with your favorite toppings such as sliced green onions, jalapenos or sour cream.

Nutritional Information Per Serving (1 bowl):

Calories; 528 Total Fats; 23 g Saturated Fat; 9g Carbohydrate 48 g Sugar 7 g Fiber 4 g Protein 29 g

ONE POT CHILI MAC

This One Pot Chili Mac is an easy and delicious meal that's sure to satisfy the whole family! It requires minimal ingredients, comes together in less than 30 minutes and will become a weeknight staple. Here's what you need:

Ingredients:

- 2 tablespoons olive oil
- 1 ¼ pounds ground beef
- ½ teaspoon onion powder
- 1 teaspoon garlic powder
- 1 teaspoon smoked paprika
- 1 teaspoon chili powder
- 1 teaspoon cumin
- ¼ cup tomato paste
- 2 cups chicken broth or vegetable broth for vegan option
- 8 ounces macaroni pasta shells or other small pasta shapes (uncooked)

How to Make:

1. Heat the olive oil in a large deep skillet over medium heat then add the ground beef, onion powder, garlic powder, smoked paprika, chili powder and cumin. Cook stirring occasionally until cooked through.
2. Add tomato paste then pour in broth followed by uncooked macaroni shells bringing mixture to a gentle simmer then reduce heat to low and let cook uncovered for 15 – 18 minutes or until most of the liquid has been absorbed by pasta and cooked al dente (firm but not overly so). Stir occasionally while it cooks if needed..
3. Serve with your favorite toppings such as sliced green onions, jalapenos or sour cream!

Nutritional Information Per Serving (1 bowl):

Calories; 528 Total Fats; 23 g Saturated Fat; 9g Carbohydrate 48 g Sugar 7 g Fiber 4 g Protein 29 g

LOADED BAKED POTATO SOUP

This creamy Loaded Baked Potato Soup is a delicious and easy weeknight meal perfect for busy families! Made with potatoes, bacon, cheese, sour cream and onion it's sure to please everyone. Here's what you need:

Ingredients:

- 2 tablespoons olive oil
- 4 slices of bacon diced
- ½ cup diced onion
- ¼ cup all-purpose flour
- 5 cups chicken broth or vegetable broth if vegan option desired
- 3 large potatoes peeled & diced into 1" cubes
- 1 teaspoon garlic powder
- ½ teaspoon smoked paprika
- ¼ teaspoon black pepper
- 1 heaping cup shredded cheddar cheese

How to Make:

1. Heat olive oil in a large deep skillet over medium heat then add bacon and onion cooking until bacon is crispy.
2. Sprinkle all purpose flour over cooked elements then slowly pour in chicken (or vegetable) broth while continuing to stir constantly until sauce begins to thicken – about 3 minutes or so.
3. Add cubed potatoes then garlic powder, smoked paprika and black pepper stirring occasionally for about 10 minutes or until potatoes are tender but still slightly firm inside (al dente).
4. Serve by spooning soup onto individual plates and top with shredded cheese if desired!

Nutritional Information Per Serving (1 bowl):

Calories; 331 Total Fats; 15 g Saturated Fat; 6 g Carbohydrate 30 g Sugar 6 g Fiber 3 g Protein 16 g

VEGAN MUSHROOM RISOTTO

This vegan Mushroom Risotto is the perfect comfort food for winter. It's creamy, flavorful and delicious. Plus, it's super easy to make in under 30 minutes! Here's what you need:

Ingredients:

- 1 tablespoon olive oil
- 1 medium yellow onion (diced)
- 2 tablespoons minced garlic
- 10 ounces mushrooms (cleaned & diced)
- 2 cups Arborio rice
- ½ cup white wine (optional)
- 5 cups vegetable stock

How to Make:

1. Begin by heating olive oil over medium heat in a large pot before adding diced onion and cooking for about 3 minutes or until tender stirring occasionally. Then add garlic followed by mushrooms – stirring gently – and cook for an additional 5 minutes before adding Arborio rice continuing to stir constantly.

2. Next pour in optional white wine if desired followed by vegetable stock then bring up to a simmer while constantly stirring every few minutes until liquid absorbs into rice – about 18 minutes or so. When done season with salt and pepper then serve warm!

Nutritional Information Per Serving (1 bowl):

Calories; 465 Total Fats; 8 g Saturated Fat; 1 g Carbohydrate 77 g Sugar 8 g Fiber 0 g Protein 11 g

VEGAN COCONUT CURRY

This Vegan Coconut Curry is a delicious and easy meal that's perfect for any night of the week. It's packed with curry powder, coconut milk and all your favorite veggies. Plus, it's ready in under 30 minutes! Here's what you need:

Ingredients:

- 2 tablespoons olive oil
- 1 medium onion (diced)
- 3 cloves minced garlic
- 2 tablespoons curry powder
- 14 ounces can of diced tomatoes
- 2 cups vegetable stock
- 1 cup coconut milk
- 1 teaspoon brown sugar (optional)

How to Make:

1. Begin by heating olive oil over medium heat in a large pot before adding diced onion and cooking for about 3 minutes or until tender stirring occasionally.
2. Then add garlic, curry powder and cook another few minutes followed by canned diced tomatoes along with vegetable stock bringing up to a simmer while constantly stirring every few minutes until liquid reduces down slightly – about 15 minutes or so.
3. Then add optional brown sugar if desired followed by coconut milk continuing to simmer an additional 10 minutes or so. When done season with salt and pepper to taste then serve warm!

Nutritional Information Per Serving (1 bowl):

Calories; 345 Total Fats; 18 g Saturated Fat; 4 g Carbohydrate 34 g Sugar 9 g Fiber 4 g Protein 7 g

VEGGIE BURRITO BOWL

This Veggie Burrito Bowl is a delicious and nutritious meal that's perfect for lunch or dinner! It's packed with bell peppers, black beans, corn, avocado and all your favorite toppings for a healthy and flavorful meal. Here's what you need:

Ingredients:

- 2 tablespoons olive oil
- 1 red bell pepper (diced)
- 1 green bell pepper (diced)
- 1 teaspoon minced garlic
- 15 ounces can of black beans (drained/rinsed)
- 8 ounces can of corn kernels (drained/rinsed)
- 2 cups cooked brown rice
- 2 avocados (pitted/chopped)

How to Make:

1. Begin by heating olive oil over medium heat in a large pan before adding diced red bell pepper and cooking for about 5 minutes or until tender stirring occasionally.
2. Then add garlic, green bell pepper and cook another few minutes before adding black beans and corn continuing to cook an additional 3 minutes or so until everything is warm throughout.
3. When done spoon ready mixture over top cooked brown rice further topping with avocado and other desired toppings such as salsa, jalapeños, cilantro, sour cream etc. before serving warm!

Nutritional Information Per Serving (1 bowl):

Calories; 390 Total Fats; 16 g Saturated Fat; 2 g Carbohydrate 52 g Sugar 4 g Fiber 11 g Protein 11 g

VEGGIE BURRITO BOWL

This Veggie Burrito Bowl is a flavorful and healthy meal that's perfect for any time of the day! It's loaded with bell peppers, black beans, corn, avocado and other tasty toppings creating a delicious and nutritious meal. Here's what you need:

Ingredients:

- 2 tablespoons olive oil
- 1 red bell pepper (diced)
- 1 green bell pepper (diced)
- 1 teaspoon minced garlic
- 15 ounces can of black beans (drained/rinsed)
- 8 ounces can of corn kernels (drained/rinsed)
- 2 cups cooked brown rice
- 2 avocados (pitted/chopped)

How to Make:

1. Begin by heating olive oil over medium heat in a large pan before adding diced red bell pepper and cooking for about 5 minutes or until tender stirring occasionally.
2. Then add garlic, green bell pepper and cook another few minutes before adding black beans and corn continuing to cook an additional 3 minutes or so until everything is warm throughout.
3. When done spoon ready mixture over top cooked brown rice further topping with avocado and other desired toppings such as salsa, jalapeños, cilantro, sour cream etc. before serving warm!

Nutritional Information Per Serving (1 bowl):

Calories; 390 Total Fats; 16 g Saturated Fat; 2 g Carbohydrate 52 g Sugar 4 g Fiber 11 g Protein 11 g

MOROCCAN CHICKPEA BOWL

This Moroccan Chickpea Bowl is a flavorful and healthy meal that's perfect for any time of the day. It's loaded with chickpeas, onions, garlic, bell peppers, tomatoes and spices to create a tasty taste of Morocco. Here's what you need:

Ingredients:

- 2 cups cooked chickpeas
- ½ cup red onion (diced)
- 1 tablespoon minced garlic
- ½ cup bell pepper (diced)
- ¼ cup grape or cherry tomatoes (halved)
- 1 teaspoon cumin powder
- ½ teaspoon coriander powder

How to Make:

1. Begin by taking medium pot over medium heat adding olive oil and diced onion stirring together until onion begins to soften before adding in minced garlic followed by diced bell pepper and chopped tomatoes while continuing to cook another 2 minutes stirring occasionally.
2. When done add in cooked chickpeas along with cumin powder and coriander powder before topping off with water bringing soups up to gentle boil reducing down afterwards.When done spoon prepared soup into bowls before serving warm!

Nutritional Information Per Serving (1 bowl):

Calories; 223 Total Fats; 6 g Saturated Fat; 1g Carbohydrate 30 g Sugar 11 g Fiber 9 g Protein 10 g

THAI COCONUT SOUP

This Thai Coconut Soup is a delicious and comforting meal that's perfect for any time of the day. It's loaded with lemongrass, garlic, ginger, cilantro, lime juice, coconut milk and spices to create a tasty flavor filled with Thai-inspired ingredients. Here's what you need:

Ingredients:

- 2 tablespoons olive oil
- 1 stalk lemongrass (minced)
- 2 cloves garlic (minced)
- 1 tablespoon fresh ginger (minced)
- 1 teaspoon ground coriander
- ½ teaspoon ground black pepper
- 2 tablespoons fish sauce
- 4 cups vegetable broth or water
- 2 cups coconut milk

How to Make:

1. Begin by taking medium pot over medium heat adding olive oil and minced lemongrass stirring together until fragrant before adding in minced garlic followed by ginger and letting it cook another minute before adding in ground coriander and black pepper along with fish sauce and vegetable broth bringing soup up to gentle boil reducing afterwards.
2. When done add in coconut milk allowing soup to heat through before taking off heat spooning soup into bowls. When ready serve warm topped with chopped cilantro leaves, green onions and a squeeze of fresh lime juice if desired!

Nutritional Information Per Serving (1 bowl):

Calories; 316 Total Fats; 24 g Saturated Fat; 18g Carbohydrate 11 g Sugar 6 g Fiber 3 g Protein 6 g

TOMATO BASIL SOUP

This Tomato Basil Soup is a simple and delicious dish that's perfect for any time of the day. It's loaded with fresh tomatoes, garlic, basil, oregano and spices to create a unique flavor. Here's what you need:

Ingredients:

- 2 tablespoons olive oil
- 4 cloves of garlic (minced)
- 1 large onion (chopped)
- 1 teaspoon dried oregano
- 2 cans diced tomatoes
- 2 tablespoons tomato paste
- ½ teaspoon sugar
- 3 cups vegetable broth or water
- ¼ cup chopped fresh basil

How to Make:

1. Begin by taking medium pot over medium heat adding olive oil and minced garlic stirring together until fragrant before adding in onion cooking another minute before adding in oregano and stirring together for another minute before adding in diced tomatoes followed by tomato paste and sugar until mixture starts bubbling. Take off heat and stir in vegetable broth bringing soup up to gentle boil reducing afterwards when done turn off heat stirring in chopped basil letting it sit at room temperature 5 minutes before spooning soup into bowls. When ready serve warm!

Nutritional Information Per Serving (1 bowl):

Calories; 126 Total Fats; 7 g Saturated Fat; 1g Carbohydrate 12 g Sugar 6 g Fiber 2 g Protein 3 g

ROASTED SALMON WITH VEGETABLES

This Roasted Salmon with Vegetables is a delicious and healthy meal that's perfect for any time of the day. It's loaded with cherry tomatoes, cucumbers, parsley, garlic, oregano, olives and bell pepper to create a tasty dish. Here's what you need:

Ingredients:

- 4 salmon fillets, each about 5-ounces, boneless and skinless
- 3 tablespoons pitted halved kalamata olives
- ½ pound potatoes cut into half lengthwise
- 2 teaspoons minced garlic
- 2 tablespoons chopped oregano (fresh)
- 1 cup cherry tomatoes
- ½ cup chopped cucumbers
- ¾ cup chopped parsley (fresh)
- ¼ teaspoon ground black pepper (divided)
- 1 medium yellow bell pepper (sliced into rings)
- ¼ teaspoon salt (divided)

How to Make:

1. Begin by preheating the oven to 425 degrees F or 218 degrees C while taking a large bowl adding potatoes oil black pepper and ⅛ teaspoon salt stirring until evenly coated before transferring mixture into prepared baking pan covering tightly with foil baking 30 minutes or until potatoes are well roasted when done.

2. Meanwhile take large bowl adding bell pepper cucumber tomatoes parsley oregano olives black pepper oil and ⅛ teaspoon salt stirring together until well combined when done place salmon fillet on cutting board sprinkling evenly with black pepper and salt rubbing until evenly coating before spooning tomato mixture over potato followed by placing salmon in middle of pan putting in preheated oven baking 10 minutes or until cooked through afterwards spooning onto serving plates serving warm!

Nutritional Information Per Serving (1 plate):

Calories; 419 Total Fats; 16 g Saturated Fat; 3g Carbohydrate 35 g Sugar 5 g Fiber 4 g Protein 33 g

VEGGIE AND CHEESE PIZZA

Total Time: 30 minutes

Servings: 2

Ingredients

- 1 cup chopped bell peppers
- ½ cup sliced onions
- 1 cup sliced mushrooms
- 1 teaspoon minced garlic
- ½ pound whole-wheat pizza dough
- ⅛ teaspoon salt, divided
- 3 teaspoons olive oil, divided
- 2 ounces torn mozzarella cheese
- 3 tablespoons grated Parmesan cheese

How to Make:

1. Begin by preheating oven to 500°F or 260°C and taking a large skillet adding 2 teaspoons of oil heating over medium before adding bell peppers, onions, mushrooms and garlic tossing occasionally cooking 5 minutes or until lightly browned before removing from heat to cool.
2. Sprinkle some flour on a clean countertop rolling pizza dough into a 12 inch circle transferring onto prepared baking tray sprinkling mozzarella followed by spreading veggies overtop drizzling with remaining olive oil before placing in preheated oven baking 10 minutes or until golden brown around sides when done afterwards spooning onto serving plates sprinkling with remaining Parmesan cheese serving warm!

Nutritional Information Per Serving (1 plate):

Calories; 468 Total Fats; 17.7 g Saturated Fat; 4.3 g Carbohydrate 50.6g Sugar 4.8 g Fiber 6.4 g Protein 23 g

STIR-FRIED RICE NOODLES

Total Time: 25 minutes

Servings: 4

Ingredients

- 8 ounces thin rice noodles
- 2 tablespoons vegetable oil
- 1 onion, thinly sliced
- 1 clove garlic, minced
- ½ teaspoon dried red pepper flakes
- ½ pound pork tenderloin, thinly sliced
- 2 cups fresh vegetables such as red bell pepper, snow peas and carrots, cut into thin strips
- 3 tablespoons soy sauce

How to Make:

1. Begin by taking a large bowl adding rice noodles boiling water letting stand 10 minutes before straining and rinsing with cold water afterwards draining out all the liquid in a colander setting aside until ready to use.

2. In the meantime, take a large skillet adding oil heating over medium heat before adding onions cooking few minutes stirring occasionally when browned add garlic & pepper flakes continuing cooking for an additional minute stirring up until fragrant.

3. Increase the heat pushing ingredients to side of skillet before adding pork slices flipping over after 3 minutes or until cooked through mixing with cooked veggies pouring in soy sauce bringing everything together allowing mixture to simmer for a few more minutes.

4. Finally, add prepared noodles tossing everything together stirring continuously for about 3 minutes or until warmed through spooning onto serving plates before serving!

GINGER & GARLIC FRIED RICE

Total Time: 30 minutes

Servings: 4

Ingredients

- 2 tablespoons vegetable oil
- 1 onion, diced
- 1 cup long grain white rice
- 2 cloves garlic, minced
- 2 tablespoons fresh ginger, grated
- 2 cups chicken or vegetable broth
- ¼ teaspoon salt

How to Make:

1. Begin by taking a large skillet over medium heat adding oil and onions sautéing until lightly browned. Afterwards add cooked rice and stirring around in the pan for several minutes before adding garlic and ginger continuing cooking while stirring all together.
2. Pour in chicken or vegetable broth bringing everything up to boil turning down heat to low simmering rice covered with lid for 15–20 minutes or until most of liquid is absorbed turning off heat letting rice stand few more minutes before fluffing up with a fork.
3. Finally spoon cooked fried rice onto serving plates season with salt if needed before serving!

Nutritional Information Per Serving (1 plate):

Calories; 241 Total Fats; 5 g Saturated Fat; 0.5 g Carbohydrate 40g Sugar 3 g Fiber 2 g Protein 6 g

CHAPTER 5 : DESSERT

STRAWBERRY FRENCH TOAST

Total Time: 20 minutes

Servings: 2

Ingredients

- 4 slices of white bread
- 1 cup sliced strawberries
- 1 tablespoon butter
- 2 eggs
- 2 tablespoons milk

How to Make:

1. Begin by taking a medium bowl and whisking together eggs and milk until combined. Afterwards take two slices of bread dip each side in egg mixture allowing excess drip off before transferring onto a plate.
2. Melt butter over medium heat once heated place the two slices of bread cooking for several minutes on each side or until golden brown colour after flipping over adding strawberries onto one slice covering with other slice pressing down lightly before transferring onto a clean plate.
3. Repeat step for the two remaining slices before serving with syrup or honey if desired!

Nutritional Information Per Serving (1 plate):

Calories; 175 Total Fats; 8 g Saturated Fat; 3 g Carbohydrate 20g Sugar 6 g Fiber 1 g Protein 8 g

BANANA PANCAKES

Total Time: 15 minutes

Servings: 2

Ingredients

- 2 ripe bananas, mashed
- 2 eggs, whisked
- 1 teaspoon vanilla extract
- ¼ cup all-purpose flour
- ½ teaspoon baking powder
- Pinch of salt

How to Make:

1. In a medium bowl, combine the mashed banana, eggs and vanilla extract until evenly mixed. Add in the flour, baking powder and salt and stir until combined. Heat a large skillet over medium heat. Grease lightly with butter or cooking spray.
2. Pour ¼ cup of pancake batter into the heated skillet for each pancake and cook for 1 to 2 minutes on each side, or until golden brown.
3. Serve pancakes with desired toppings such as syrup, fruit or whipped cream. Enjoy!

Nutritional Information Per Serving (1 plate):

Calories; 175 Total Fats; 4 g Saturated Fat; 1 g Carbohydrate 21g Sugar 13 g Fiber 1 g Protein 8 g

MAPLE BUTTERSCOTCH COOKIES

Total Time: 25 minutes

Servings: 2

Ingredients

- 1 ½ cups oat flour
- ½ cup dark brown sugar
- ¾ cup maple syrup
- ½ teaspoon baking powder
- 1 teaspoon cinnamon
- ½ cup unsalted butter, melted
- 4 ounces butterscotch chips
- ¼ cup almond milk, unsweetened

How to Make:

1. Preheat the oven to 350°F (175°C). Take a large baking sheet and line with parchment paper. In a large bowl mix together dark brown sugar, maple syrup, baking powder, and cinnamon stirring until evenly mixed.
2. Then add melted butter to the mix whisking until it is evenly distributed. Add in milk and oat flour blending together until everything is fully incorporated.
3. Finally add butterscotch chips into the mixture and stir until all pieces are evenly spread throughout. Scoop 2 tablespoons of batter onto prepared baking sheet leaving enough space between each cookie.
4. Place the pan in preheated oven for 15 minutes or until golden brown color is achieved. Let cookies cool down for 10 minutes at room temperature before serving them onto plates enjoy!

Nutritional Information Per Serving (1 plate):

Calories; 313 Total Fats; 17 g Saturated Fat; 11 g Carbohydrate 31g Sugar 18 g Fiber 2 g Protein 3 g

APPLE CINNAMON MUFFINS

Total Time: 25 minutes

Servings: 4

Ingredients

- 1 cup all-purpose flour
- ½ cup almond flour
- ¼ teaspoon baking powder
- ¼ teaspoon baking soda
- ¾ cup coconut sugar
- ¾ teaspoon ground cinnamon
- 2 apples, peeled and diced in small cubes
- ½ cup vegan butter, melted
- ½ cup almond milk, unsweetened

How to Make:

1. Preheat the oven to 350°F (175°C) and take a 12 cup muffin tin and line it with paper liners or grease with vegan butter. In a large bowl add flours, baking powder, baking soda, coconut sugar and cinnamon stirring until fully mixed.
2. Then add melted vegan butter and mix until evenly combined before adding almond milk blending everything until evenly mixed again.
3. Lastly stir in diced apples making sure that each piece is properly coated with the batter before spooning into prepared muffin tin. Place it in preheated oven for 15 minutes or until golden brown color is achieved.
4. Let Muffins cool down for 10 minutes at room temperature before serving them onto plates enjoy!

Nutritional Information Per Serving (1 plate):

Calories; 193 Total Fats; 11 g Saturated Fat; 6 g Carbohydrate 21g Sugar 16 g Fiber 3 g Protein 3 g

CHOCOLATE BANANA MUFFINS

Total Time: 25 minutes

Servings: 4

Ingredients

- 1 cup all-purpose flour
- ½ cup almond flour
- ¼ teaspoon baking powder
- ¼ teaspoon baking soda
- 3 ripe bananas, mashed
- ½ cup vegan butter, melted
- ½ cup cocoa powder, unsweetened
- ¾ cup coconut sugar or other dry sweetener of your choice

How to Make:

1. Preheat the oven to 350°F (175°C) and take a 12 cup muffin tin and line it with paper liners or grease with vegan butter. In a large bowl add flours, baking powder, baking soda, coconut sugar and cocoa powder stirring until fully mixed. Then add melted vegan butter mixing until evenly combined before adding mashed bananas blending everything until evenly mixed again. Lastly spoon the batter into prepared muffin tin placing it in preheated oven for 15 minutes or until golden brown color is achieved. Let Muffins cool down for 10 minutes at room temperature before serving them onto plates enjoy!

Nutritional Information Per Serving (1 plate):

Calories; 211 Total Fats; 11 g Saturated Fat; 6 g Carbohydrate 27g Sugar 22 g Fiber 3 g Protein 2 g

CHOCOLATE COCONUT PANCAKES

Total Time: 25 minutes

Servings: 4

Ingredients

- 1 cup oat flour
- ½ cup almond flour
- ¼ teaspoon baking powder
- ¼ teaspoon baking soda
- ½ cup vegan butter, melted
- ½ cup cocoa powder, unsweetened
- ¾ cup coconut sugar or other dry sweetener of your choice
- 1 cup almond milk, unsweetened
- ⅓ cup shredded coconut

How to Make:

1. Preheat the oven to 350°F (175°C) and take a 12 inch skillet or large bowl mixing together flours, baking powder, baking soda, melted vegan butter and cocoa powder stirring until fully combined.
2. Then add coconut sugar before stirring in almond milk and shredded coconut blending everything until even.
3. Take the prepared mixture pouring 2 tablespoons of batter onto preheated skillet letting it cook for 1 minute on each side or until golden brown color is achieved. When done take pancakes off the stove, place them onto plates and enjoy!

Nutritional Information Per Serving (1 plate):

Calories; 310 Total Fats; 19 g Saturated Fat; 8 g Carbohydrate 29g Sugar 22 g Fiber 5 g Protein 6 g

CARROT CAKE PANCAKES

Total Time: 25 minutes

Servings: 4

Ingredients

- 1 cup oat flour
- ½ cup almond flour
- ¼ teaspoon baking powder
- ¼ teaspoon baking soda
- ½ cup vegan butter, melted
- ½ cup carrot puree, unsweetened
- ¾ cup coconut sugar or other dry sweetener of your choice
- 1 cup almond milk, unsweetened
- ⅓ cup shredded coconut, unsweetened

How to Make:

1. Preheat the oven to 350°F (175°C) and take a 12 inch skillet or large bowl mixing together flours, baking powder, baking soda and melted vegan butter stirring until fully combined.
2. Add in carrot puree before stirring in coconut sugar and almond milk blending everything until even. Take prepared mixture pouring 2 tablespoons of batter onto preheated skillet letting it cook for 1 minute on each side or until golden brown color is achieved.
3. When done take pancakes off the stove, place them onto plates and enjoy!

Nutritional Information Per Serving (1 plate):

Calories; 310 Total Fats; 19 g Saturated Fat; 8 g Carbohydrate 29g Sugar 22 g Fiber 5 g Protein 6 g

MANGO COCONUT ICE CREAM

Total Time: 20 minutes

Servings: 3

Ingredients

- 2 ripe mangoes, peeled and diced
- ¼ cup coconut milk
- ½ teaspoon vanilla extract, unsweetened
- 1/3 cup agave syrup or other sweetener of your choice
- ¼ cup shredded coconut, unsweetened

How to Make:

1. Take a medium bowl mixing together diced mangos, coconut milk, vanilla extract, agave syrup and shredded coconut stirring until everything is fully blended.
2. Take the mixture pouring it into an ice cream maker turning it on following with manufacturer instructions or until desired consistency is achieved.
3. When done take ice cream out of maker placing it onto plates before serving it.

Nutritional Information Per Serving (2 scoops):

Calories; 140 Total Fats; 5 g Saturated Fat; 0 g Carbohydrate 27g Sugar 24 g Fiber 1 g Protein 2 g

TOFU SALAD

Total Time: 10 minutes

Servings: 4

Ingredients

- 2 blocks extra firm tofu, drained and cubed
- ¼ cup vegan mayonnaise
- 3 tablespoons vegan sour cream
- 1 tablespoon apple cider vinegar
- 1 teaspoon Dijon mustard
- ½ teaspoon garlic powder
- ¼ teaspoon black pepper
- 2 stalks celery, diced
- ¼ cup pickles, diced

How to Make:

1. Take a large bowl adding the cubed tofu, vegan mayonnaise, vegan sour cream, apple cider vinegar, Dijon mustard and garlic powder stirring until everything is evenly combined.
2. Into the same bowl add celery and pickles blending everything together until everything is coated. Place in refrigerator for 15 minutes before serving cold over salads or crackers.

Nutritional Information Per Serving (1/4 of the recipe):

Calories; 189 Total Fats; 13 g Saturated Fat; 3 g CarbohydrateD 8g Sugar 5 g Fiber 3 g Protein 11 g

BBQ TOFU

Total Time: 10 minutes

Servings: 4

Ingredients

- 2 blocks extra firm tofu, drained and cubed
- ¼ cup vegan BBQ sauce
- 1 tablespoon olive oil
- ½ teaspoon garlic powder
- ¼ teaspoon black pepper, ground

Instructions

1. Preheat oven to 375°F (190°C). Next, add cubed tofu to a baking dish before covering with vegan BBQ sauce ensuring everything is evenly coated.
2. Drizzle olive oil over the top followed by sprinkling garlic powder and black pepper before placing in the preheated oven for 15 minutes or until desired texture is achieved. Serve hot and enjoy!"

Nutritional Information Per Serving (1/4 of the recipe):

Calories; 91 Total Fats; 5 g Saturated Fat; 1 g Carbohydrate 6g Sugar 3 g Fiber 2 g Protein 8 g

Made in the USA
Coppell, TX
28 August 2023

20908428R00039